THE *Path* TO A PEACEFUL HEART

THE *Path* TO A PEACEFUL HEART

Tearing Down the Walls of Childhood Trauma and Finding Freedom, Understanding, and Purpose

Taylor Tagg

The Path to a Peaceful Heart: Tearing Down the Walls of Childhood Trauma and Finding Freedom, Understanding, and Purpose

Praise for Taylor Tagg and *The Path to a Peaceful Heart*

"I know Taylor Tagg as a man of principle with a heart of gold. He is a skilled and caring guide to the experience of a peaceful heart. His book shines with sincerity, knowledge, and faith in the healing process. With gentle authority gained from his own courageous journey of healing childhood trauma, Taylor encourages us to step on to the path, and go all the way to peaceful resolution of our worst stories. If you're ready for a long-awaited change inside, this beautiful book will be your friend along the way."

Mary Hayes Grieco
Author, *Unconditional Forgiveness*
www.maryhayesgrieco.com

"This book will touch your heart and change what is possible for you in your life. It is heartfelt, engaging and truly inspiring. Taylor offers a path to healing our wounds from the past and provides the steps to how we can each live a more peaceful, loving and fulfilling life. Thank you for having the courage to change and extend that gift to us."

Dorothy Lazovik
President of Authentic Leaders Edge, Inc.
www.authenticleadersedge.com

"If past traumas plague you into adulthood, The Path to a Peaceful Heart is the prescription you need to follow in order to let go! Life seldom hands us an eraser, but this book demonstrates how to release the pain and replace it with peace. It is a blessing of a book!"

Judy Williamson
Director of the Napoleon Hill World Learning Center at Purdue University Calumet
www.naphill.org

"Taylor's honesty, integrity and deep wisdom shine through! These qualities not only define Taylor as a cherished friend and colleague, but also as an outstanding professional forgiveness mentor. His PEACE process is a rational forgiveness program with great heart - an open door to a lifetime of freedom and happiness."

Elizabeth Lewis
Licensed HeartMath Provider
Stress Management & Life Coach
www.elewishealingarts.com

"Taylor has taken severe challenges and used them to give hope to people suffering in their lives. He leads the reader through a process that deals with and uses life's challenges for the greater good. This book has the potential to drastically change people's lives."

Tom too tall Cunningham
Napoleon Hill Certified Leadership Instructor
www.tom2tall.com

"Taylor's style is smooth and easy to read. It's very straightforward and obviously from the heart. I went for years thinking I'd been dealt a bad hand and would have to learn to live with it. Taylor's book was a big help."

Edie Marshall
Memphis, TN

To Adversity and Defeat, thank you for being my greatest teacher

The Path to a Peaceful Heart

Acknowledgements

I would like to thank all of the people who contributed to my story and who continue to be my biggest champions. A big thanks goes to my wife Sherri, I'm very grateful for your love and support; to my mom, thank you for dedicating your life to my well being; to my dad, thank you for the eternal gift of faith;

To Michael Kelberer, thank you for helping me dig deep to bring up the painful details; to Joy Jacoway, thank you for showing me how to bring creative expression to my story; to Mary Hayes Grieco, thank you for continuing to be my spiritual mentor and Master example of Forgiveness; and to Judy Williamson, thank you for supporting me immensely through the work of the Napoleon Hill Foundation.

A very special thank you goes to all those who have shown me love and kindness, especially Edwin and Sarah Hughes. Your gift of unconditional love saved my life.

To Dr. Napoleon Hill, your thirteenth principle of success kept me hanging in there for what was possible, long after possible had seemingly checked out of my life. Thank you. To Father Joseph L. Tagg, III, thank you for showing me the Path to a Peaceful Heart and lighting the forgiveness torch in me. It burns brightly within my soul.

Lastly to the reader, thank you for allowing me to share my message.

I am so very humbled, grateful, and honored to spend time with you and expand the ever important work of Forgiveness in the world.

In Lasting Peace and Unconditional Love,

Taylor Tagg
September 2012

Chapter One – The Beginning of My Healing Journey

I'll never forget the day my childhood came flooding back to me.

I was pulling into my parking space at FedEx, coming to a stop in my white 1997 four door Nissan Maxima. It was hot that morning, and the air conditioning was barely keeping my sweaty legs cool against the warm black leather.

I was thirty-three years old, working for the high-powered transportation giant as an accountant, and ready to begin another go get em' day on the job. I had Journey's "Only the Young" blaring out of the Bose speakers and out of the blue I was suddenly hit with a tidal wave of emotion and a barrage of scenes from the Dan days.

For the first time ever, I saw the ten years of abuse in their totality.

The memories rolled over me like a tsunami. I relived, for the first time as an adult, just how horribly my mom and I had been mentally and emotionally abused by this man.

All the senseless repetition of his phrases, the crazed yelling and screaming about his sexual needs, the invective and vulgar cussing at us, the intense anger on his face and the terror we felt as a result; the not knowing if tonight was the night one of us got badly hurt, the relentlessness of the ten year emotional onslaught – it all came roaring to the surface.

"Holy Mother of God," I thought, "WE WERE ABUSED!"

I sat in my Maxima stunned.

I felt like a concrete statue. I couldn't move.

Many times as a child I felt like that. I would stand frozen, like I had been blasted with a stun gun as Dan adjusted his bottle rimmed glasses enough to take a deep breath and shout at the top of his lungs about how inept and inadequate my mom and I were as human beings.

I also realized that morning as I sat in my car with the engine off, sweating all the way through my Brooks Brothers button down shirt, just how deeply I had buried all my emotions from that period.

It was as if my feelings about life had lain dormant in a coffin for years.

I had made good resolutions about moving forward in my life, but I had resolutely kept a closed lid on the past.

I came to an understanding in that car that you can't analyze an abusive situation while you are in it – you learn to get through each present day and, if you wake up the next morning, go through the next. All the hurtful feelings, the cumulative oppression, you block out and stuff down.

So that moment in the FedEx parking lot was a major step forward for me. Not only did I vividly re-experience what had happened to me as a child,

I acknowledged it by giving it a name: Terrible Undeserved Abuse.

Chapter Two – What The Trauma Was Like For Me

I was a blond haired, blue eyed kid with a heart of gold and a good basketball jump shot. I loved life and generally, I was happy as a young child.

However, I didn't build a life of confusion, heartbreak and victimhood by accident. I was taught by an expert.

My life of victimhood started when I was ten years old. With my parents divorced, my father took a job that kept him mostly out of town. My mom had her hands full raising me by herself. Even at a young age, I could tell she was struggling to provide for us.

One day an old high school acquaintance of hers (let's call him Dan) entered our lives with the promise of financial security. We didn't realize at the time that the price of that security included a steady diet of emotional and verbal abuse, a family culture of blame and shame, and the terror of frequent and unpredictable raging tantrums.

My mom and I happened to bump into Dan while shopping at a clothing store in Memphis. They exchanged phone numbers. Dan called her and came over to the house one day.

For whatever reasons, my mother was open to what he was presenting, and he started coming over on a regular basis.

Dan was a relatively short man, 5'7" with perfectly parted grey hair and thick brass rimmed glasses. He had a muscular build and was neatly dressed. He had good handyman skills and a knack for getting jobs done.

At first, things seemed quite positive. Dan looked for ways to be helpful wherever he could. He also provided needed financial help, which relieved a lot of stress for my mother.

He would often pick me up after school and give me a ride to the house where he would wait for my mom to come home from another hard day's work fielding customer service calls for FedEx.

After a few short months, the dark side of Dan began to emerge. At first there was a gradual increase in yelling, from once in a while to once a day to once an hour. His tone of voice became angry and penetrating in harshness.

His sentences became short phrases and rhetorical questions that required no response, and he would repeat these phrases over and over again like a broken record, "The cat got your tongue? The cat got your tongue? Huh? Can't you speak? Can't you speak? Huh? Huh? Huh!

As the frequency ramped up, so did the intensity. Eventually, the yelling and incessant repeating of phrases evolved into explosive rage and unyielding harassment.

Dan would erupt with anger at the drop of a dime, obsessively repeating his words with a crazed frenzy in his eyes and pent up fury running through his veins. Even though most of this screaming was directed at my mother, I was often in the room and terrified.

Over time, the content of his yelling got nastier and nastier. He used disgusting language and every cuss word in the book.

If you can think of anything vulgar or debasing, it was said in that house. Most often it involved a detailed description of what Dan's sexual needs were.

I listened to and absorbed every word.

I was shamed to the core of my being because I accepted the explicit language as if he was talking to me too.

Dan was predictably unpredictable. He worked at a prison, which seemed to exacerbate and encourage his sudden bursts of rage.

You were just as likely to get a nice, "how's it going?" from him as you were a demented, "your mother won't give me what I want."

Then he turned to her, "isn't that right mom? Huh? What's wrong with you, you stupid whore! When are you going to give me what I want?! HUH? HUH!"

I also found myself becoming a yeller, and not just to Dan. One day, when my mom asked me to do something I didn't particularly want to do, I snapped, "Why don't YOU do it you crazy bitch!"

For a few seconds, I could feel the adrenaline. An intense surge rushed through my veins, I was DAN!

I felt extremely powerful. And then my mother pointed her finger at me and said, "Don't you ever in your lifetime speak to me that way again."

And my ego-bubble burst.

After I berated my mother, I really started to understand at a basic level what was happening in my home, that Dan was not just a painful presence, but a corrupting one.

I felt ashamed.

I felt a sadness I can't describe.

I thought about running into the bathroom and throwing up. I was sick to my stomach.

I had taken Dan's words and actions as my own and my mom helped me realize it.

I resolved that day to never, ever act like Dan again.

My mother usually defended herself to Dan by yelling and screaming back at him (although not using the language). We soon learned that all her reciprocation did was fuel the fire that was blazing. What we did or said was never good enough.

Our words were faithfully met with increased resistance and harassment from Dan. This level of communication was a shock to my young system at first, and it took a long while for that shock to wear off.

We also tried defending ourselves through silence. When Dan was doing his toxic volcano thing, we would simply not respond.

Like all playground bullies, though, Dan was into it for the reactions: he wanted and needed to see fear and subservience, and above all, reactions. Our silence just made him work harder.

I said that Dan's invectives were usually hurled at my mother, but sometimes, if my mother didn't react the way he wanted, he'd shift over to me.

One night, Dan was getting good and worked up. He had run the gamut of his vulgarity dictionary, trying to get my mother and me to react. He had harassed her enough that night that I just wanted to crawl into a hole forever.

But, his antics weren't getting the response he wanted. They were going in one ear and out the other.

In a last, desperate effort, Dan snarled his lips, pointed at me, and yelled mightily at my mom, "WHY DIDN'T YOU JUST ABORT HIM!"

That hurt. Bad.

Adrenaline surged throughout my body and I got very angry. I felt like my skin had been set on fire. I just wanted to react and punch him in the face.

I was in such shock and shame I was unable to utter a single word, and all I could think in my mind was, "Deal with it Mother F.....er! I AM HERE NOW!"

I was thirteen.

We did on many occasions try to get help in protecting ourselves from Dan. We tried calling the police, but he'd take off before they arrived and come back right after they'd left.

As you might imagine, this did not have the effect of calming him down. More than once, my mother got an actual court restraining order against him, but that didn't do much good either. He'd manage to be gone when the enforcement arrived, and that was as far as it went.

We tried locking the door against him. It would work for awhile, but then he'd literally kick the door down. We felt terror as we heard the lock snap and saw the door buckle. Dan would then roll in twice as full of rage as normal. Trying to keep him out of the house turned out to be worse than expected, and more expensive, so we quit this tactic as well.

Looking back on those years from the present, I can see how I evolved robust mental and emotional defenses against the constant misery and threats.

As a young, budding fourteen year old teenager, my defense had definite tendencies of fantasy.

One night, when I just couldn't stand his rants anymore, I decided that if I couldn't physically remove Dan from the house, I had to come up with some other way to deal with him.

I decided to make sure he didn't find me inside the house. I needed to feel like a winner for once.

So, I hid in a dark corner of the back den. It was 9 PM and no lights were on in the room, so it was hard to see. I pretended I was invisible, that Dan couldn't see me no matter how hard he looked.

The hiding space in the corner of the den was small and very narrow. It provided just enough room for me to crouch down like a baseball catcher between the wall and a light oak workstation. "This space will be perfect," I thought as I gently moved my feet back and forth on the hardwood floor to test the sound in case I lost my footing.

The feel in the air was thick as I took my position in the corner. "Tonight is my night," I said softly.

I would not move again for quite awhile.

It took Dan one hour to notice my absence. I began hearing his footsteps as he quickly started looking for me in the other rooms of the house. All the while, I was confidently nestled in that corner, now fatigued and aching, but never moving as much as a finger.

The only parts of my body that I moved were my eyes.

I had complete confidence that Dan wouldn't find me. I had been through enough. I was so determined to do something to relieve the insanity of the pressure, I felt like my life depended on it.

I created a sharp image in my mind of a highly paid, top tier espionage pro. I was serious. I had skills. I had a career here!

After some more rumbling, I heard Dan come to a stop. He had finished searching all of the other rooms and he was beginning to panic. From a distance I heard him say, "Where is Taylor!"

There was only one room he hadn't checked yet: the back den.

I'll never forget the loud click of his loafers against the hard maple wood as Dan approached the back den. I thought, "Here we go. This is it."

He walked with authority into the middle of the dimly lit space and scanned the wood paneled room from right to left. A lamp that was on in the front of the house shined softly back into the middle area of the den, providing some indirect light that did not reach to the four corners of the room.

My back was glued to the wall. I squatted motionless in the back left corner.

As he peered into the opposite parts of the room, his head moving slowly around towards me, I decided to hold my breath.

I suddenly noticed the air in the room was hot and stagnant. I started to sweat. I had to be so very still.

There was a deafening silence as my weakening legs began screaming in pain. As Dan's line of sight got closer and closer to me, he seemed to look more intensely.

"Please not tonight," I thought.

Finally, Dan peered directly into the back corner where I sat frozen. He let out a slight grumble of frustration, and proceeded to walk right out of the den.

As I heard the click, click, click of his shoes moving away from me, I exhaled slowly. I made a silent fist pump. Victory! Success!

Then I heard my mom telling him that I had run out of the house to the police station. That sent Dan into an all out panic. He bolted out the backdoor and into the night.

That time in the den was a breakthrough in my development for two reasons.

I used the power of my mind for the first time as an approach to successfully get what I wanted.

Finally, I found something that worked! That night I was on top!

Second, by hiding successfully, I thoroughly rewarded myself for being invisible.

Little did I know that I would use hiding as a way of life for many more years to come.

As I got older, my defenses evolved as well. As a full on teenager, I would see Dan coming, his blood curled face screaming obscenities, but I was no longer a part of the chaos mentally.

I'd go to a place called Tune Out City.

It was a place up in my mind, far away from the present, and it was a workable solution to the pain I was experiencing. I had to get away from the harassment whatever it took.

As it turns out, I became a little too happy living in Tune Out City.

Apparently, I became the beloved mayor of that town. As I moved through late childhood and into adolescence, I journeyed further into Tune Out City and farther away from reality.

I walled off my heart so no one could enter and no feelings would see the light of this dangerous world. My move to Tune Out City did a lot to protect my heart during those years, but it couldn't prevent the slow drip of animosity and deep emotional resentments from forming.

The other defense I developed was Blame.

I developed the conviction that I had all the answers and could blame everybody else for what was wrong in my life. Nothing could be my fault because I had all the solutions.

And I'll tell you – it felt unbelievably good. I felt superior.

Since I could do no wrong, I could solve everyone's problems if they would only let me tell them how they can straighten their act up! I believed I was right and I had the standard for living that everyone else should follow.

Blame and righteousness were brilliant disguises that allowed me to hide my toxic shame completely from view.

Eventually, the actual trauma came to an end, and I began to awaken to the fact that my two defensive strategies, while they worked in the short run, had long-term toxic effects as serious as the abuse itself.

Not only that, those toxins were buried deep, and they weren't coming out without a fight.

Chapter Three: Awakenings

The end to the physical ordeal was anti-climatic.

I graduated from high school and was two years into college, staying in Memphis but moving out of my house and into a dorm room on campus. I thought about going further away for school, but something in me wouldn't allow it. I felt I needed to stay close to mom so that I could get home quickly if something went terribly wrong.

One day, completely out of the blue, she told me, "He just stopped coming over. Dan's not coming back." She said she didn't know why and I certainly couldn't figure it out.

To be quite honest, I don't think either of us had the energy to care. It was just over and we were relieved.

Ten solid years of yelling, screaming, harassment, tantrums, breaking doors down, calling the cops, restraining orders that did no good, and hiding were over.

It was like a switch had been thrown: one day, yes, next day, no more.

But of course, it was just the physical part that ended. The mental and emotional scars were deep-set and lingering.

Of course, some healing did take place fairly soon after Dan left. For example, even after I left home I still found myself waiting for overreactions from people, anticipating that at any given moment that the person I was with would fly off the handle and start ranting.

Although it rarely happened in reality, it wasn't until after I got the news of Dan's departure that I finally actually noticed that those overreactions weren't, in fact, happening in real life.

After Dan left I began to notice that there was, in fact, a relative peace and quiet all around me.

These realizations required a significant mental adjustment from me. I had to learn to accept the peace and quiet as the new normal, and, even harder, to react in kind.

Not long after these realizations, I had another real mental breakthrough. The totally foreign thought occurred to me, seemingly from heaven, that I, William Taylor Tagg, Jr., of Memphis, Tennessee had the power to choose how my life would move forward.

First, I chose right then and there not to EVER become like Dan.

I was absolutely never going to inflict upon another person what had been so unjustly inflicted on me.

Second, I realized that I could actually choose what to do with my life. I don't think I had realized up until then just how trapped by Dan's presence I had felt.

With him gone, the sky became the limit. I could work where I wanted, live where I wanted, get married if I wanted, and have kids if I wanted. I could BE NORMAL!

The day I activated the power of choice in me was one of the truly special days of my life. Just like that, life suddenly had amazing possibilities again.

I knew deep down the heavens handed me the golden key to one of life's greatest secrets. I felt so humbled and excited at the same time!

I was twenty years old.

But once the headiness of that realization passed, I realized that something still wasn't right. In fact, looking back, a lot still wasn't right; I just couldn't see it yet. I wasn't ready to see it yet.

But a series of major awakenings took place, spaced over several years that finally brought me from a life of denial to one of seeing reality. These awakenings were the first crucial steps on the Path to a Peaceful Heart.

Awakening #1: The Real Taylor Tagg is Revealed

After college, and exercising the aforementioned power of choice, I made my way into home ownership and life in the corporate world. I began to settle down a little bit.

I was twenty four years old and taking life by storm. I was in firm control of my fate, or at least it seemed that way. I had a good job, good life, nice car, and ... and then the first time bomb left over from the Dan days went off.

I'll never forget that day. I woke up one morning, my teeth were clinched, and I was MAD AS HELL!

I thought, "Wait a minute. I don't have one good reason to be this mad." My temper had been a problem at times, but I couldn't think of anything that was actually happening in my life that had gotten me upset. For no good reason, I was just really, really angry.

I thought I needed to look into this anger more, but I didn't know where to go with that thought. So, I just let it fall by the wayside.

Around this same time, I came to realize that I really wanted a girlfriend in my life. I started to date around a little bit, but nothing stuck, and I seemed to be having trouble meeting women. A few years passed, and I finally managed to get into an on-going relationship with a very nice woman named Kathryn.

I was pretty excited about the relationship and thought things were great when all of a sudden (it seemed to me), she ended it. It took me by total surprise, so I asked her: "What's the deal? Why the breakup?"

She said, "Taylor, you are a great guy, kind, sweet, and loving. BUT, I don't know you at all."

Kathryn went on to tell me that she couldn't figure out where I stood on much of anything, I certainly didn't express my feelings directly about things, and that without being able to see inside me, she couldn't be in a relationship with me.

No sooner had she finished talking when I was blindsided with a *monster flash of insight*. In that moment, I saw clearly that every one of my relationships had ended the exact same way, with variations on the same explanation: "This is great, Taylor, you are a fabulous guy and we have fun, but I don't know you or how you feel."

I was stunned and numb.

This was not an "Aha" moment; it was panic-stricken "Uh oh" moment.

This revelation hit me at the core; I couldn't stuff it or wish it away.

It hurt deep down; in fact, it stung far worse than the breakup itself. It hurt because I knew inside that I *wanted* to be known, I *wanted* to be emotionally open, I *wanted* that intimacy and I *wanted* it really, really badly.

And in that moment, I saw that I couldn't open up, and I had no idea how to begin.

I looked at myself in the proverbial mirror, and realized I was staring right at the problem.

Click!

It registered in my brain and more importantly in my heart.

I AM the problem! I AM the dang problem!

I could see clearly how completely locked down emotionally I was, how unworthy I felt. I saw through the blame game I had been playing and realized how terrified I was for people to actually see the real me.

I literally went into a drop-out-of-the-sky tailspin for exactly three weeks. I was extremely vulnerable and emotionally wide open. I would walk down the street and for no apparent reason just burst into tears.

I had no control over my emotions.

I did the best I could while just surrendering to the roller coaster. It was one of those upside down, spin you sideways rides too.

Toward the end of those three weeks, though, another awareness began to emerge. I felt that a major core shift was starting to take place within me.

The real Taylor Tagg was slowly coming to the surface. Who was he? I didn't know. I just knew that all of the hiding, yelling, screaming, and blame that I thought once defined me wasn't me at all.

Truth be told, I was on that emotional roller coaster because the false identity of having all the answers, being right, and having the top standard for living suddenly fell away.

At the drop of a dime, *I had no answers. I wasn't right about anything. I wasn't the standard for living, only my own standard.*

I realized everyone else had their own ways for living that were best for them. I had to look at my naked truth.

I felt totally exposed, but somehow I knew I activated a reset button on myself. I had no superiority left to draw on. It hit me that I was just one small person among many, but with my own unique talents and gifts.

The security blanket of authority I relied on all my young life was gone.

Poof. I felt tremendously lost.

I was literally a blank slate and I was scared to death.

The first concrete step I took was to see a psychologist. It took a lot of courage for me to do that because it meant I had to talk about me. When you've been told that you don't matter for so long, talking about yourself feels like nails being dragged on a chalkboard.

I said to myself, "who cares about my words? My thoughts? Who the heck am I?"

There weren't a lot of tangible results for a while. Despite the few steps and insights, I was still somewhat in denial. It took me awhile to get used to being so open and brutally honest with myself.

However, just being in that conversation helped fertilize the ground for the next couple of steps forward in my story. I realized that there was hope out there. I had no idea who I was, but I trusted that now I could choose who I wanted to be.

I just needed to find the right path.

Awakening #2: The End of Denial

If there was any denial left over for me to conquer, it ended that morning in my Nissan Maxima as all of my childhood memories came flooding back.

Once the shock of the returning memories wore off, I unstuck my sweaty microfiber khakis from the leather seat and gingerly walked inside to continue to make sense of what had happened. As I staggered into the office, I realized that two major pieces of my puzzle had converged.

The first piece was realizing that I was in fact the facilitator of all the problems I was having in my adult life.

The second piece was connecting those problems back to the ten years of unrelenting abuse I experienced throughout my adolescence.

With blame off the table as an excuse and my naked truth out in the open, it was high time I had a deep, internal look at me. I began this step by resolving to give up two very important positions.

The first position I resigned from was being a perfectionist. In my own blame game, I created a subpersonality of the perfect me who could do no wrong. That persona was extremely taxing and difficult to live up to. In my mind, I was always the dictionary. If someone pronounced a word wrong, I would be the first one to correct him or her.

Being a perfectionist pushed me to obsessively refine my life, not allowing so much as a moment of accomplishment to enter my heart. I felt like I would become soft if I celebrated anything. Doing well was just "expected." I didn't cherish successes. I increased my standard instead.

Because I felt like a failure trying to get Dan out of the house on many occasions, my self-esteem plummeted as a result. I was relentlessly trying to be successful in any and every aspect of my life. I felt very much in control this way. I also became inflexible and wanted all things done with the mentality of "my way or the highway."

Nothing ever was good enough for me because I never felt like I was good enough. In the end, I learned that doing your very best with what you have is what counts!

It was a huge relief to finally release the perfectionist in me and fully accept in my heart that excellent effort and success were perfectly adequate.

The second position I gave up was a lot larger responsibility...General Manager of the Universe. With the perfectionist in me falling away, I gave up trying to be everything to everyone. Because I had not been rescued as a little boy, I had made it my job subconsciously to rescue everyone around me in need.

I tried so hard to do for others what was never done for me. I dated many women who had been in bad relationships or had issues with one of their parents specifically to comfort them. I felt compelled to help them. I was meeting them at their level of pain because mine was still pretty raw too.

While doing the General Manager job well, I sacrificed my own needs to feel important in this way. *I discovered in the end that no one needed rescuing, only me.*

Chapter Four: Solutions

Forgiveness

Growing up, I had an uncle, Joe Tagg III, who was a Catholic priest and whose primary message centered on Unconditional Love and Forgiveness.

He made the case (he was a lawyer too!) for why we should forgive people based on it being the highest form of Love. Now, his message of forgiveness was very persuasive and although at the time I didn't think much of it intellectually, I realize now that I had taken his core message to heart.

After the parking lot incident, the thought came to me: Maybe forgiveness is what's needed here. I certainly wasn't interested in forgiving Dan for his sake, but would it help me?

From deep down, the answer came back: YES!

So, I gave it a try. I just closed my eyes, asked God for Divine intervention, took a deep breath, and just let Dan's hold on me go.

I visualized a hole opening in my chest (that's where I hold pain) and I visualized my hands pushing the memories out. I pushed out and away the energy of those feelings from my body.

I saw clearly that I had unconsciously been holding on tight to my feelings toward Dan, and even holding on to the trauma itself, as if it was an integral part of me. Now I was letting all that go.

I had another "random" thought, and sat down and wrote Dan a letter. In it, I cussed him out up and down and then sideways for making our lives so painful. Who did he think he was!

I wrote all my stored up feelings about him on paper, four or five pages worth of truly marvelous, let er' rip venting.

Then, I burned the letter and watched it turn to ash. And, in a surprising moment of inspiration, I mentally sent Dan good intentions and love for his soul.

With those two inspired actions, I forgave Dan for all the years of hurting my mother and me. As the forgiveness sunk in, something wonderful happened.

Suddenly, I felt tremendously better and lighter. I cracked a smile on my face that ran the width of the state of Tennessee. A channel of light seemed to open in my heart.

That felt INCREDIBLE! Whew! Wow! YES!

It was a heck of a moment.

I still remember it vividly. Forgiveness freed me.

As it turned out though, that moment, as beautiful as it was, was not the end of the pain or the journey.

There was more work to do, one last step that turned out to be the best part of all – the "problem is me" part.

Self Forgiveness

Although the predominant feature of my childhood was those ten years of pain and heartache, there were some good parts that, as it happened, were the seeds of my healing and growth. I've already mentioned my uncle and the crucial learning about forgiveness.

Another nurturing seed was my exposure as a little child to unconditional love in its truest form. Many of us have a grandparent or special person that just loves us for everything we are and are not, the proverbial warts-and-all kind of love.

This gift came to me from my Granddaddy and Grandmother Hughes. They lived several hours away and I would visit three or four times a year, spending the summers with them while I was out of school.

They loved me without conditions and judgments as a child, something I was extremely fortunate to experience given my daily exposure to its exact opposite. If Dan was my devil, my grandparents were my angels.

After I forgave Dan and some time went by, I began to be aware deep down I wasn't finished with my journey. I was also aware, once again, that I didn't know what else to do.

And, once again, I solved that immediate problem by sending up a request to the Universe asking it to reveal to me the Next Step.

I said to the Heavens, "I'm ready to move on. I need the missing piece."

It's funny how real-life events are set into motion by the seemingly "unreal" acts of asking for help.

I was apparently good and ready to complete the Path to a Peaceful Heart.

Very soon thereafter, I came across an online video of Brene Brown talking about shame and how it greatly affects a person's life. Her video touched me and spoke to me in a very immediate and intimate way.

I wondered if this was the piece I was missing.

I wanted answers fast, so I went back to the psychologist to talk about shame. I soon discovered that there was indeed a tremendous amount of personal shame I was holding on to.

It was hidden from my conscious mind.

I had no idea I was harboring toxic humiliation and embarrassment.

I learned how toxic shame can run our lives. We acquire it by quietly and subconsciously taking responsibility for situations in our childhood that we clearly have no responsibility for.

Shame hooks in through the simple question of, *"What did I do wrong?"*

Without any explanation or answers, we internalize shame and take it as our own, which carries over with us into adulthood. It causes unbelievable internal conflict and strife in our lives as we replay our childhood tapes over and over.

Toxic shame is a silent epidemic in the world.

Millions of adults are harboring this shame and they don't even know it. They continually protect hidden core wounds that create great suffering from subconscious childhood responsibilities that were never theirs in the first place.

My psychologist suggested that I go back to a specific time in my life when I was a little boy and write down what I saw.

So one day, I sat down at the dining room table in my home and made an intention to visit the little boy that once was me.

A vision came to the surface right away.

I saw an anguished faced, eleven-year-old boy standing at the side of our house looking down the driveway. He was sweltering in another hot and humid Memphis summer afternoon.

He scratched his nose against his red and white striped shirt as his light khaki shorts draped down to his mid thighs. He pulled his dirt stained white socks back up to his knees and loosened the shoe strings on his dark blue tennis shoes.

This little boy looked scared and alone. I saw him lean against the house to escape the pressure that the unyielding concrete had on his sore feet. As he winced, his confused expression suggested he had waited a very long time, as if someone had far since passed the period to come pick him up.

He appeared to be utterly defeated.

As I gazed compassionately at this child with my adult eyes, I understood clearly that little Taylor had subconsciously accepted the role of "the man of the house" because he wanted to be helpful as all kids do.

But while he took on the job of being the man of the house, he failed in every way at what he saw as his most important duty: trying to get an abusive man out of his mother's house.

I could see that he couldn't possibly have had the physical strength, the emotional fortitude, or the experience to win that battle. He was dealing with a grown, mentally sick man.

But little Taylor didn't have the benefit of my adult eyes, so that little boy in me was doomed to feel like a failure from the start.

Shame set in. The really toxic kind.

I stayed with the vision of little Taylor, watching him standing alone and afraid outside, quietly waiting for someone to come get him and take him away from all that mess. His young face looked so miserable, and he was desperate to be rescued.

With that image fresh in my mind, I wrote that little guy a letter of apology acknowledging his struggles.

I visualized my adult self going back to that grey driveway and walking with purpose up to the scared fella. Little Taylor knew immediately who I was and why I was there.

I put my arm gently around his small shoulder, brought him snug into me, and comforted him.

Then I said with a gentle voice, "Taylor, thank you for your efforts. Your work here is done. I have come to take you away from this place forevermore. You are safe with me now."

Tears flowed down my cheeks as little Taylor looked up at me with his big blue eyes and an incredibly grateful sigh of relief.

He hugged me tightly. The sense of connection between me and my younger self was extraordinarily powerful and visceral.

I started shaking uncontrollably and taking in several deep breaths. I suddenly felt extremely weak, but with every exhale, I seemed to be releasing years and years of poisonous shame.

I cried really hard.

In that beautiful moment of emotional release, the thirty-year-old self-imposed walls of toxic shame came crashing down into a pile of ash.

As the proverbial dust settled, I noticed that my heart opened up and for the first time in a long time, *I was without something.*

It took a few minutes to sink in, but then I realized that something was the heavy burden, pain, suffering, abuse, perfectionism, righteousness, low self-esteem, non-acceptance, and fear of failure I had carried.

It was gone.

And then the peace flowed in.

It was a deep, strong, thought-free, sacred stillness that tasted like an ice cold drink going down your throat on a sweltering summer's day.

Aaaahhhhh...

This peace was not a fleeting moment, but an inner, lasting knowledge that all played out the way it was supposed to.

I felt that now I was on the other side of pain and suffering.

I felt calm and very light, 100% tension free, and very grateful to be alive.

In that moment, I saw the infinite beauty in all things around me. That feeling was utterly amazing.

And just like that, I knew I was finished with my suffering for good. In short, I forgave and released myself from the burden of failure from my childhood to the present.

I felt that younger me journey away from that traumatic past and become reunited with the present.

As I did, the monstrosity of the thirty year ordeal instantly shrunk to the size of a ping pong ball.

In my mind's eye, I could see the whole journey in its entirety, from start to finish. It was miraculous!

Energy in me that had been stuck for thirty years began flowing again.

As a full and unbroken man for the first time, I was able to completely accept what had happened to me, and was able to let go of the expectation that my childhood could be, or would ever be, any different.

I realized from a deep place that this pain was placed in my life so I could overcome it.

I believe now that the Universe speaks to us all through heartache and pain. No one is exempt.

It's what you do with it that counts.

Chapter 5 – Preparing for the Journey

"In every adversity, every disappointment, every struggle there is a seed of equivalent benefit waiting on you if only you will look for it."

~ Napoleon Hill

I believed that statement with all my heart and held on to what it could mean in my life one day, and that's what created the PEACE process.

PEACE bloomed into freedom, understanding, and purpose.

As you begin your own PEACE Process, start with believing that peace will happen, have a willingness to feel uncomfortable feelings, know that time is with you, and activate faith that a Peaceful Heart will be yours.

Believe peace will happen for you.

You can do this! If you think you can't, then you must. It took me thirty years of feeling around in the dark, searching, crying, wanting anything better than feeling like a victim. I've shortened this process for you by decades. You can and you will find peace.

That state of mind begins with believing it can happen. When you believe, you activate the part of your brain that will make it possible for you to get through your pain and find peace.

Activate Faith in yourself and put it into action. This is very important! Believe peace will happen.

Feel the feelings.

This process will bring up negative feelings from the past. Those of us who have suffered abuse have coped with these negative feelings in a myriad of ways: drugs, alcohol, other forms of substance abuse, manipulation, and a million ways to numb our senses.

Don't blame yourself for this – burying those feelings was a necessary (and successful!) strategy to protect your younger self. But now, allow your heart to feel the hopelessness, despair, and whatever else comes to the surface. The key to peace is to feel the pain and eventually (through the PEACE process) let it go for good.

You must grieve the loss and feel the feelings that you have hidden for so long. It is the single most important thing you can do to keep your feet centered on the Path to a Peaceful Heart.

Know your journey is a marathon rather than a sprint. Your journey is a marathon for a reason.

As you walk through the healing process, you will gain new positive perspectives that you will slowly integrate into your life. These integrations take time, but are well worth the effort to pace yourself utilizing your unique rhythm of life.

Lastly, be brave. Activate Faith.

The key to achieving a truly Peaceful Heart is not to bury the pain, but to take the necessary steps to transform it.

There are beautiful gifts waiting for you, buried deep in the heart of your suffering, right where it hurts the most. These gifts have been there since the beginning, and are just patiently waiting for the day you will journey within and find them.

Put them to use for your greater good and for the greater good of humanity. No matter how far down the well of trauma you've fallen, the journey back up will always be good and nurturing.

"But I will write of him who fights and vanquishes his sins, who struggles on through weary years against himself and wins."

~ Caroline Bigelow Lerow

The Path to a Peaceful Heart PEACE Process

Practice becoming an Observer Witness

Examine Your Repeating Pattern

Apply Choice

Claim Your Freedom through Forgiveness of Another

Elevate Your Heart and Soul through Forgiveness of Self

Believe, Feel, Forgive, Activate!

Chapter 6: The Five Step PEACE Process

"Amazing. Simply amazing!" That was my thought the day I rescued the eleven-year-old Taylor standing in the driveway. Peace of Heart Day for me was March 11, 2011.

I turned around in my mind that day and looked back at the whole trauma experience as if I had just finished watching a long movie.

I was stunned to realize that the whole process from start to peace took thirty years, almost to the day.

Here I was, one month from turning forty, and three quarters of my life had been hijacked by that trauma in one way or another.

And now, astonishingly, I was finally free of it.

I've spent a lot of time since then thinking about what the process was that brought me from a state of complete emotional shut down to a fully functioning adult experiencing Peace of Heart today.

The first thing that became obvious was that I had been trying to get from Point A to Point Z without a map, so the real-life journey for me took a long time and felt pretty random.

What I've done is distill that random, messy process down into a clear roadmap for reaching Peace of Heart from the starting point of childhood hurt and pain.

If you follow this roadmap, I believe that you, too, can be free of the prison walls you have been living behind for years. And, because you'll be going into the process intentionally, and with guideposts along the way, I'm betting you can be free of those prison walls a lot quicker than I was. [Note – but please don't rush it – everyone has their own journey, their own best pace!]

This heart-centered system is about regaining mental, physical, emotional, and spiritual health.

For many, the PEACE process will be a complete life-changer. For others who have already traveled along the path, it will shed some light on what they already have accomplished, and where they may need to go from there.

For everyone that takes this process to heart, they will have an internal cleansing of the spirit and soul, backed by the tremendous power of forgiveness.

Forgiveness is something most of us are unwilling to do, but the benefits for those who take this step are nothing short of miraculous. So please – keep an open mind.

When the road gets tough, be reminded that each one of us is proactively choosing to go down this transformational path.

In the words of Victor Frankel, who both physically and emotionally survived the Nazi death camps,

"Between stimulus and response, there is a space. In that space lies our freedom and power to choose our response. In our response lies our growth and freedom."

Step #1 to Peace of Heart – Practice Becoming an Observer Witness

This can be a tricky step, because while you need to gain some objectivity in order to survive, if you get too much objectivity, you can swing over to an equally unhealthy state.

In the throes of my pain, I was in complete agony. I felt intense suffering from the nightly verbal and emotional assaults, and I needed relief.

I heard someone say on television, *"Don't take things so personally."*

I instantly connected with that statement and did my best not to take the yelling and screaming to heart.

Overnight, I went from the victim of the trauma to the observer witness of it.

In my mind, the trauma was over there somewhere, and I was standing right here, emotionally not a part of it any longer.

So far so good, but I went even further.

As the mayor of Tune Out City, I was no longer emotionally present for anything in my life.

I learned later that this kind of complete dissociation is often the last, desperate tactic of trauma victims trying to protect themselves from intense pain.

I was just trying mentally to survive, but I paid a heavy price for the completeness of tuning out. I disassociated all the way to the point that I stuffed all feelings beyond recall. I became emotionally unavailable in all of my relationships.

To this day, I'm still working to be fully present emotionally.

Having said that, some separation is needed.

Get to a place where you accept that the situation is what it is regardless of how you feel about it. Only 2% of human kind ever clearly understands this distinction.

The separation came for me when I realized and accepted that I was more than my emotions. You are a higher presence as well, with and without reactions.

Because you are a higher presence, the ability to consciously choose your response in any circumstance rests fully under your control.

First, look at the situation. Then see how you feel about it.

Now, set aside your feelings for a minute, and just look at the *facts*.

Creating separation is an eye opening experience and a completely necessary preparation for Step 2.

Here are two ways to create that space as an *observer witness*:

- For short term relief, and as a way to start, try this: when you feel your emotions rising out of control, take a timeout, ascend to a 10,000 foot view, and try to describe what's happening to you starting with the words, "How interesting...."

  Like this: "How interesting it is that every time my mother refuses to react to her abuser's vulgarities, he brings me into the yelling."

  Or this: "How interesting it is that my abuser always tries to hurt my mother by cussing at me."

  It may take a few trials, but keep at it.

- Then, when you feel a little confidence that you can take this a little deeper, try this:

  Imagine you are sitting in a dark movie theater watching a giant screen and the movie about to play is of you and the story of your trauma.

  Now imagine going up to the movie room where the film plays. Get behind the glass.

You are surrounded by walls and glass and nothing can get to you. Or if you are more comfortable, sit in your seat in the theater and imagine a bubble totally surrounding you.

Inside that bubble you are safe.

No one can enter without your permission.

Now, look at your life playing out on the big screen as if you were watching someone else other than you.

Let go of all expectations you have of yourself.

Watch without reacting, without judging, without doing anything.

Imagine you don't know the person up there. Close your eyes and play the story.

What do you see?

How did it seem without the expectations?

If you had to give a report on this person you "didn't know", what would you say about the person objectively?

Now that you have seen your story through an observer witness lens, did this create a little breathing room between you and your story?

Remember this space is non-reactive and non-judgmental.

All you need in the beginning is a tiny crack in the armor. That crack will get larger the more you practice it.

Before you know it, you can get tremendous perspective by looking at yourself and the characters in your own movie with an objective lens, totally pulled back and unplugged without feeling toward it one way or another.

In the immortal words of Joe Friday: "Just the facts, ma'am."

Step #2 – Examine Your Pattern through a Self-Inventory

I had my first breakthrough when it dawned on me that all of my relationships were ending the same way.

That's when I finally got it.

It had been years since my abuser was any physical part of my life, and yet here I was still acting the same way as if he was standing right next to me.

I saw that the problem and the solution were now inside of me, and not "out there."

I saw that I wouldn't let anyone get close to me, and I refused to get close to anyone else. The intense shame that was created by the abuse had been internalized as my fault, and persisted long after the actual abuse ended.

My belief about myself was, "You are nothing and not worth getting to know. Don't let anyone get close to you."

This self-inventory can be a tricky step for those who have suffered through childhood trauma, for three reasons.

First, we have a natural revulsion at the thought that any responsibility for what's wrong in our lives belongs to us.

We were the victims! We were just kids, for crying out loud!

Second, the mere act of looking at ourselves is often extremely painful, because of that toxic shame we experienced for so long.

Third, looking at ourselves feels like a slippery slope toward letting the abuser off the hook for his crimes, and we definitely feel major resistance toward that!

The self-inventory is awkward but necessary.

For now, use the insights you gained from creating separation between yourself and the trauma to:

1. **Look objectively at what's happening in your life now.**

   More specifically, what's not working for you?

   What is the pattern that keeps repeating?

   What part do you play in this pattern?

   For me, having any kind of sustained relationship was a major part of what was not working.

I continually placed blame on my girlfriends to avoid my toxic hurt and make myself feel better.

I was able to pull back and objectively see that to get what I wanted, I had to take responsibility for my actions and put the blame towards others down.

2. **Separate your current behavior from the source of the pain.**

For me, I had to realize that what wasn't working in those relationships was me, not my abuser. My abuser had been gone for years.

He established the pattern of blaming my mom for everything.

I took that pattern as my own and repeated it over and over throughout my life.

The source of the pain was the little boy in me feeling like a failure.

In order to avoid that acute suffering, I blamed everyone else through my words and actions. I didn't take responsibility for me. That compromised my closest relationships in every way.

3. **Look at how much your current life is still being dictated by the abuser:**

   a. How much of my behavior towards others is treating them the way the abuser treated me?

      In my case, I was still playing the blame game, shifting responsibility to my abuser, to the women, to anyone but me.

   b. How much of my opinion of my own self worth (and the worth of others, for that matter) is based on the internalized messages I received from my abuser.

      I felt, deep down, that I was not worth knowing. At worst, I believed that if anyone could see the real me they would be repulsed.

      So I kept the real me locked up in a deep, deep dungeon.

4. **Let go of blame.**

I had to not only stop blaming my abuser for what was broken in my life, I had to stop blaming myself too. I had to give myself a much needed break.

Blame is born of shame and keeps us a prisoner of the past. What we're after is simply acknowledging what is happening in the present, and looking at the facts without discoloring them with shame and blame.

Having someone you trust to talk this stuff through with can be a big help.

It's always easier to gain some objectivity on a subject when you have to try to explain it to someone else.

Looking at yourself is hard, but keep the end in mind: **Peace of Heart!**

Step #3 – Apply Choice by Taking Your Power Back

There was no doubt in my mind, after I took the Step 2 self-inventory, that my current life was still greatly affected by the pain of my childhood.

I still felt like a powerless product of my past, forever doomed to be broken and alone.

While I was in the midst of the trauma, I blamed my abuser. I also secretly blamed myself for not being able to do something about it.

After my abuser departed my life, I continued the pattern, always blaming other people and circumstances for whatever wasn't working in my life. As long as someone else was to blame, that meant I had nothing to do with it.

In a way that felt good.

But one day after taking that self-inventory, like a parting of the clouds, I had the epiphany that I had choices in life.

I realized that there was no one who could do anything about what was happening in my life besides me.

I was my only ticket to sound mental health.

As long as I kept blaming others, I had no power in my life.

I gave my power away.

And with that epiphany, I began to take my power back.

My past I couldn't change. But the present and future were in my hands.

It was a very powerful and exhilarating moment.

I changed from a lost ship adrift at sea to the captain of my ship, the deliverer of my destiny. My sails might be tattered and broken, but I had the power to sail that bad boy anywhere I pleased.

I decided to accept 100% responsibility for my life and everything in it, good and bad.

I also acknowledged that I contributed on some level to bringing the abuse into my life as well.

Having reclaimed the power of choice, I was empowered to take the biggest and most important steps of all: coming to terms with my abuser, and coming to terms with my childhood.

Step #4 – Claim Your Freedom through Forgiveness of Another

"The Path to a Peaceful Heart is found only through these three words...ALL IS FORGIVEN."

~ Father Joseph L. Tagg, III

There's only one technique for finally closing off your toxic connection to your abuser: forgiveness.

No, it's not letting the abuser off the hook. It's not about giving the abuser something he or she doesn't deserve.

In fact, forgiveness is not about the abuser at all.

The true essence of forgiveness is letting yourself off the hook – the hook of the toxic shame and fear that is eating your present self alive.

It's not about giving the abuser freedom from the consequences of his or her actions; it's about giving YOURSELF the freedom from the consequences of the abuser's actions.

For me, this process did not come easily, and it was some time after the idea of forgiving my abuser came into my head that I eventually forgave him for the years of undeserved trauma in my life.

When I was ready, it became clear that I had yet another choice:

I could continue to harbor the shame and guilt, or I could forgive and move on.

I chose to move on.

I let go of the expectations I harbored about him, that he would somehow, magically, do my past differently and do the right thing, stop the harassment, and make things right.

In fact, flush with the power, I even mentally sent my abuser good wishes in my heart for his own healing.

I also forgave my mom.

As a child, I simply did what she did. I yelled and screamed along with her until I realized the error of my ways. I know now that my mom did the best she could with the tools she had.

In talking with her about the ordeal, she was not aware of the deep lingering effects the abuse had on me.

My mom also felt a terrible sense of shame because she wasn't able to get her abuser out of our house. She was surprised to learn that, as a child, I mirrored her every move and every word, absorbing every little nuance of her, both good and bad.

I just did what she did. She awakened to the truth of how powerfully her actions affected the quality of mine.

I let go of all blame towards my mom.

The forgiveness process I used to forgive her and my abuser was a little messy but effective. It went like this:

- I sat down in a comfortable chair and imagined my abuser sitting on the other side of the room.

  I took a few deep breaths. I thought, "maybe I need to forgive him today."

  After a few moments, I stated my intention.

  "I think I will forgive him today."

- Then I proceeded to vent about the abuse. I told him exactly how I felt.

  I allowed myself be selfish for once.

  This wasn't fair play – this day was all about me. I got my true feelings out into the open so I could let them go.

  I took a long time with this part, as long as I needed to get it all out on the table.

- When I was done, I sat in silence and acknowledged that the totality of the abuse had nothing to do with me, and everything to do with him.
- Then I gave all the responsibility for the abuse back to him.

  I said: "I'm not carrying this stuff anymore. It's all yours now."

- I released the expectations that the abuse and everything that surrounded it would ever be any different than it was.

  I told him sitting across the room: "It was what it was. You didn't do the right thing. You did what you wanted to do. However, I'm not going to blame you anymore. I'm done with that. I'm letting this go for good."

- Then I said these words with heartfelt compassion,
  "I forgive you and I forgive all of it."

  A couple of minutes later, I felt a positive energy, power, and freedom coming in to fill the space inside my spirit that I just created by letting go of all that stuff.

- Finally, I wished my abuser well in finding healing for his life.

I said, "I hope you find peace and healing somehow for yourself."

Once I was done, I sat quietly for a few moments and savored the feeling of being a victim slipping away for good, and the feelings of acceptance, gratitude, and aliveness filling my heart.

I felt better about what I did, and as a result, I let this process become more and more a part of me over the next several days.

Not long after this, I discovered a clear cut method of forgiveness in *The Eight Steps to Freedom* found in the work of Mary Hayes Grieco.

Mary is the author of *Unconditional Forgiveness: A Simple and Proven Method to Forgive Everyone and Everything*, and the director of The Midwest Institute for Forgiveness Training in Minneapolis, MN.

I saw a lot of similar important elements in her step by step method as the ones I had stumbled upon instinctively.

I have been very influenced by her work ever since.

Eight Steps to Freedom: How to Forgive Another

From *Unconditional Forgiveness* with permission by Mary Hayes Grieco

Prepare for Change in Your Life

Step One: State Your Will to Make a Change

Step Two: Express Your Feelings Exactly as They Are Inside You

Step Three: Release Expectations from Your Mind, One by One

Step Four: Restore Your Boundaries

Step Five: Open Up to the Universe to Get Your Needs Met in a Different Way

Step Six: Receive Spirit's Healing Energy into Your Personality

Step Seven: Send Unconditional Love to the Other Person and Release Him or Her

Step Eight: See the Good in the Person or Situation

Integrate Your Change and Start Living in a New Way

You can learn more about Mary's *Eight Steps to Freedom* at www.forgivenesstraining.com.

Step #5 – Elevate Your Heart and Soul through Forgiveness of Self

Forgiving my abuser was a huge relief for me, but after the initial good feelings wore off, I realized I was not done with my journey.

In hindsight, I realized that I still was not totally at peace with myself. And somehow I knew deep down that I had to learn to love me.

I saw that I was still treating myself the way I had been taught by my abuser.

I was always my own worst critic, even cussing myself out on a number of occasions, repeating over and over exactly what my abuser had done to me. I was experiencing the double whammy effect, living the trauma twice.

The final step on the Path to a Peaceful Heart happened for me when I went back (via letter) and rescued that little boy in the driveway. I wrote a letter to that child, forgiving myself for trying to be a man in a boy's body.

I felt compassion for little Taylor taking responsibility for an intolerable situation without the tools to be successful.

Writing the letter to the little person in me was one of the most freeing exercises I've ever experienced in my life.

It gave me permission to release the past and heal my core wound deep down.

After I wrote the letter, I stopped resisting my hurt and let go of all the burdens, sorrow, and hiding. The little boy in me was safe now, which had not been the case for the better part of thirty years.

I had reached the point where Taylor, the small child, and Taylor, the adult, became one being who was at peace through the power of forgiveness, compassion, acceptance, and unconditional love.

Here's the **Step 5 Self Forgiveness Process** I used to write the letter, forgive myself, and come to terms with Little Taylor:

- I pictured an image of my younger self (Inner Child), and listened with compassion as he told me what it felt like to be left behind and hurt.

  I listened carefully and specifically picked up on energy of the shame and guilt that I felt from Little Taylor.

- I released my expectations that my past would have been different. This also meant that I let go of my expectations that I would ever be "normal," i.e. someone without an abusive childhood.

- I forgave my adult self and my younger self for everything that occurred.

  With compassion, I reminded both of my selves that I did the very best I could with what I had at the time.

- I reached out to my younger self, apologized, put my arm around that child in a loving and protective embrace, and let myself know that the adult me is taking over the job of keeping my younger self safe and secure.

I told my younger self that everything will be okay now, his work is finished.

- Finally, I let go of my own shame and guilt by embracing my past - the real one, full of abuse and trauma – as a necessary but painful series of trials and triumphs that created the wonderful and unique human being that I am today.

  I allowed my heart and soul to see what was good about me as a result of everything I endured.

Mary Hayes Grieco's *Steps of Self Forgiveness* are also very effective, similar, and inspirational.

Visit www.forgivenesstraining.com and read her chapter on self-forgiveness, which explains these simple steps in greater depth.

Five Steps of Self Forgiveness

From *Unconditional Forgiveness* with permission by Mary Hayes Grieco

Step One: Prepare Yourself to Make a Change

Step Two: Talk out Your Problem with Your Higher Self

Step Three: Connect to Higher Self and Lift Yourself to Its Level of Consciousness

Step Four: Grant Yourself Forgiveness from this Higher Level

Step Five: As Your Personal Self, Give Thanks for the Forgiveness and Perspective

Working the first three steps to the PEACE Process brought me out of the hurt, but it was through the power of forgiveness that I found Peace of Heart.

It was (and is!) awesome beyond words. I had never been able to even conceive of a day when I would feel like a full person, but it was now upon me and I was free, free as an eagle to soar on to other accomplishments and successes.

And because a true act of forgiveness really seals off the past once and for all, I know that I will never have to go back to that dysfunction ever again.

By paraphrasing the words of the great Dr. Martin Luther King, I couldn't have said it any better than this:

"I am free at last. I am free at last. Thank God Almighty, I am free at last."

The Path to a Peaceful Heart PEACE Process

Practice becoming an Observer Witness

Examine Your Repeating Pattern

Apply Choice

Claim Your Freedom through Forgiveness of Another

Elevate Your Heart and Soul through Forgiveness of Self

Believe, Feel, Forgive, Activate!

Chapter 7– Your Moment of Decision

As best as I am able, I've told you truthfully what happened to me in my childhood and the lasting effects the trauma had on my adulthood.

The pain was agonizing and undeserved. Even when the actual abuse ended, the defense mechanisms I developed to survive the abuse continued to rule my life.

I remained imprisoned behind the walls of Fortress Tagg, emotionally unavailable either to myself or others.

I had no idea for a long while that I was being held prisoner. Once I had that awakening, I had no idea how to escape.

Learning how to break free was the ultimate challenge.

The dysfunctional part of me was hard to let go of. It was grounded in the illusion that I wouldn't make it, that I wouldn't get anywhere beyond broken.

This illusion whispered softly in my ear over and over again that I had no chance, no ability to conquer the very thing that had conquered me during my most pivotal, growing, and informative years.

I completely believed that I didn't have a chance of coming through all the confusion with any sanity left. It took decades for me to fully realize and understand the impact that this abuse – and the illusion it created – had on my brain.

This illusion was so powerful that even after my awakenings, even after I realized that the illusion had imprisoned my soul, I was very reluctant to give it up.

That illusion seemed to have its own instinct for self-preservation.

It would have been much easier to just quit searching for an answer. I had every reason on this planet to say, "It's just not in the cards for me. I'm just going to have to live with this and take what life gives me."

The illusion had me where it wanted me. It kept me in the perfect position to fail and keep on failing, and I did just that for quite a long while.

The tide turned when I found Choice.

I simply chose to keep looking for an answer, any answer that was just slightly better than what I had.

Somewhere deep down, in the very recesses of my soul, somewhere so deep it seemed beyond the bottom, that first act of choice ignited a glimmer of hope.

It reminded me that somehow, one day before I was old and grey and my belt buckle was pulled up around my chest, I might have the intelligence and luck to figure out this trauma puzzle.

I kept searching and persevering.

I had no idea, not even a clue to a clue of how it could happen. I just knew that someway peace could happen and I hoped I was around when it did.

Over a long period of time, I learned exactly what I needed to, and not too long ago, freedom and peace became mine.

I won the crucial battle against the dysfunctional part of me. The past no longer has a hold on my present or my future.

That thirty year period of my life will forevermore be a part of me. But now I can truly look back on it and appreciate how valuable it was in creating the person that I am today.

I am strong, loving, patient, open, compassionate, forgiving, and peaceful. Now, when I look in the mirror I am very, very grateful.

The golden key to my success was discovering how to transform those thirty years of suffering into something useful.

That something useful is helping fellow victims of childhood trauma, and one outcome of that decision was the writing of this book.

I've also shared with you my own story of *healing*.

I hope that it gives you inspiration to recover from the hurt that scarred your childhood and still today operates in the background of your adult life.

Everyone can live a fully engaged life.

We all can live every day with a Peaceful Heart.

Here is some final guidance as you begin your journey. Three things will almost certainly happen along the way that will try to sabotage your success:

People around you will resist

As you begin your new journey of Peace and Tranquility, there will be roadblocks. You may have people around you that love you just the way you are and they want to keep you that way.

They probably don't mean any harm, but they will resist change in you because they aren't ready for you to change.

You will kindly have to let those people know that change for you is good now and the timing is right. Tell them to be prepared to change with you. Some will and some won't. However, expect resistance.

Count on it to happen.

You will resist

The Path to a Peaceful Heart is not the easiest. Yet, it will be easier than you think because you are ready. However, you still need to be prepared to meet setbacks, doubt, apprehension, and fear.

No one ever makes a positive, core change in their life without coming face to face with these challenges.

Remember my persistent illusion that I wouldn't get beyond broken?

Instead of getting discouraged, look at the setbacks, doubt, and fear as teachers designed to see if you are really ready for change.

This perspective makes the results much sweeter because you endured them and stayed the course.

So, expect fear to knock on your door. Do the odd thing and invite it in. Look at it square in the face and know there is a higher side of you that wants Peace more than anything else in life. Overcome your fear by walking right through it.

The Path is about progression, not the destination

Keeping the end in mind, enjoy the process of discovery along the way, good and bad. This journey is about the progression not the destination.

The entire PEACE process will reveal layers of details that are meant to be absorbed and appreciated by your heart and soul.

Make sure to notice and take those details in: *All of them.*

Cultivating the virtues of patience and trust can greatly ease your journey to peace. Trust you will get there, and notice the small changes and shifts along the way.

When it doesn't go your way, be patient.

This is important.

The small changes you see in your journey are the building blocks for the transformation you are seeking. Enjoy the little successes; be forgiving of the minor setbacks.

When you feel negative feelings rise up after a step backward, shift your feelings by asking yourself, *"What am I learning from this step backward? What has allowed me to leap forward?"*

Pay attention to these answers.

Let me restate how important it is to go on this journey with a knowledgeable, trusted confidant.

In my opinion, the best option here is a professional who specializes in helping victims of childhood pain. Please take the time to find someone.

Be strong, be steadfast, and be determined.

What I can promise you is that if you stay the course, you will be rewarded beyond all your expectations.

I know that when I began my journey, what I wanted was pretty limited because I did not believe I deserved much more than "limited."

However, when the peaceful heart finally came, it brought with it an unparalleled feeling of freedom and relief.

- *A Peaceful Heart* brought warmth back into my soul. In forgiving my abuser, my heart has reopened as a direct result.

- *A Peaceful Heart* brought warmth back into my heart. I've been able to come out of hiding and actually give and receive love with everyone around me. I'm no longer perpetually alone and lonely.

- *A Peaceful Heart* brought self-acceptance. I was able to see myself for the person I had become, but also for the person I could be. I learned to accept and then love the child I was, and move with confidence toward the man I am becoming.

- *A Peaceful Heart* brought lasting inner peace. The last piece of the puzzle fell into place when I went back and reconnected with that poor, terrorized young Taylor. I gave him the long overdue love and security he needed, and re-united him with my present, adult self.

- *A Peaceful Heart* brought purpose. As the peace worked its magic on my heart, I felt a deep urging to help others who have been through difficult times achieve the peace we all deserve.

This moment of decision is yours for the taking. Decide right now that you want Peace of Heart in your life forever!

Trust that the "PEACE that passes all understanding" will come.

It did for me. It will for you.

About Taylor Tagg

Taylor worked in Corporate America for twenty years as a Senior Accounting and Finance Advisor.

He understands the value of assets and liabilities and it is no coincidence that he now helps people reframe their deepest personal struggles into their most productive triumphs.

Taylor aims to serve you as a professional guide as you start your own journey to peace.

Schedule a free Peaceful Heart coaching session with him to talk about where you are and what you're next step may be.

Phone: 901.921.8901

Email: ttagg@TheEvolvingHeart.com

Additional ways to work with Taylor:

- Book Taylor to deliver the PEACE Process as a Keynote Speaker
- PPH Private Coaching, Virtual Coaching, Phone Coaching
- The Path to a Peaceful Heart Home Study Course
- The Path to a Peaceful Heart Companion Workbook

You can reach Taylor by phone, email, or through the web:

Phone: 901.921.8901

Email: ttagg@TheEvolvingHeart.com

Blog & Website
http://www.TheEvolvingHeart.com

Please utilize the free Evolving Heart Emotional Management Tools on the Web and sign up for The Path to a Peaceful Heart Newsletter!

Social Media

Like Us on Facebook:
http://www.facebook.com/ThePathToAPeacefulHeart

Follow Us on Twitter:
http://www.twitter.com/taylortagg

Connect through LinkedIn:
http://www.linkedin.com/pub/taylor-tagg/2a/bb9/61b

Suggested Reading

Unconditional Forgiveness, Mary Hayes Grieco, 2011.

The Keys to Success – 17 Principles of Personal Achievement, Napoleon Hill, 1997

The Gifts of Imperfection, Brene Brown, 2010

The War of Art, Steven Pressfield, 2011

Power vs. Force, Dr. David R. Hawkins, 2002

The Power of Intention, Dr. Wayne Dyer, 2005

You Can Heal Your Life, Louise Hay, 1999

Enrich Your Sunrise, Taylor Tagg, 2003

"In every adversity, every disappointment, every struggle there is a seed of equivalent benefit waiting on you if only you will look for it."

~Napoleon Hill

www.ingramcontent.com/pod-product-compliance
Lightning Source LLC
LaVergne TN
LVHW020649100826
845148LV00012B/2401

* 9 7 8 0 6 1 5 6 9 1 6 3 3 *